Desert Plants

Ernestine Giesecke

D0890725

Heinemann Library
Chicago, Illinois

Designed by Depke Design
Illustrations by Eileen Mueller Neill
Printed and bound in China by South China Printing Company.

10 09 08
10 9 8 7 6 5

Library of Congress Cataloging-in-Publication Data

Giesecke, Ernestine, 1945-
    Desert plants / Ernestine Giesecke.
        p. cm. – (Plants)
    Includes bibliographical references (p.   ) and index.
    Summary: Describes how various plants adapt to life in the desert,
including the prickly pear cactus, sagebrush, and Indian blanket.
    ISBN 1-57572-821-4 (lib. bdg.)   1-4034-0527-1 (pbk. bdg.)
    ISBN 978-1-57572-821-6 (HC)   ISBN 978-1-4034-0527-2 (Pbk.)
    1. Desert plants—Juvenile literature. [1. Desert plants.]
I. Title. II. Series: Plants (Des Plaines, Ill.)
QK938.D4G54 1999
581.754—dc21   98-44523
                                                              CIP
                                                              AC

Acknowledgments:

The Publisher would like to thank the following for permission to reproduce
photographs:
Cover: Dr. E.R. Degginger
Susan E. Degginger/Dr. E.R. Degginger pp. 2, 14; Dr. E.R. Degginger pp. 4, 15-
16, 19-20, 22, 27; Victoria deBettencourt/EarthScenes p. 5; Richard and Susan
Day/Earth Scenes p. 8; Rich Reid/Earth Scenes p. 9; Frank Burek/Earth Scenes p.
10; Willard Luce/Animals Animals p. 11; Dr. E.R. Degginger/Earth Scenes p. 12;
Stephan Ingram/Earth Scenes p. 13; Richard Shiell/Animals Animals p. 17; Patti
Murray/Earth Scenes p. 18; Dr. E.R. Degginger/Earth Scenes p. 21; Kenneth R.
Morgan/Earth Scenes p. 24; Ted Levin/Earth Scenes; p. 25; Jim Steinberg/Photo
Researchers p. 26; Richard Kolar/Earth Scenes p. 28.

Some words are shown in
bold, **like this.** You can find
out what they mean by
looking in the glossary.

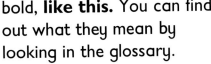

CAUTION!

**Be careful when you visit the desert. Always take an adult
with you. Be careful what you touch—the spines on many
plants can be very painful.**

Contents

The Desert

Some deserts are sandy. Other deserts are rocky or stony. One desert may be sizzling hot. Another desert may be freezing cold. But all deserts have one thing in common. All deserts are very, very dry.

Deserts get very little rain during a year.
The rain they get disappears quickly.
Plants and animals that live in desert
areas must be able to live for a long time
without water.

Desert Plants

Saguaro Cactus

Prickly Pear Cactus

Sagebrush

Barrel Cactus

Brittlebush

Plants that grow in deserts are able to survive with very little water. These plants have **adapted** to the very dry conditions.

Joshua Tree

Cholla Cactus

Creosote Bush

Mexican Gold Poppy

Indian Blanket

Each kind of plant has a special way of getting and saving the little water that is available.

Prickly Pear Cactus

The prickly pear cactus is a **succulent** plant. It has thick, **fleshy** pads. Each pad is shaped like a pear. The pads help the plant store water.

The pads of the plant are covered with sharp spines. The spines keep desert animals from eating the fleshy leaves.

Cholla Cactus

Most plants lose water through their leaves. This cholla (choy-a) cactus, like other cactus plants, does not have leaves. It has sharp needles. The needles lose less water to the air than leaves would.

The silver spines on some cactus plants help **reflect** sunlight away from the cactus's trunk. This is another way the cactus keeps cool.

Saguaro Cactus

The saguaro (soo-WAR-oh) cactus grows very slowly. A plant that is fifty years old may be just thirteen feet tall. A large saguaro can be home to woodpeckers and owls.

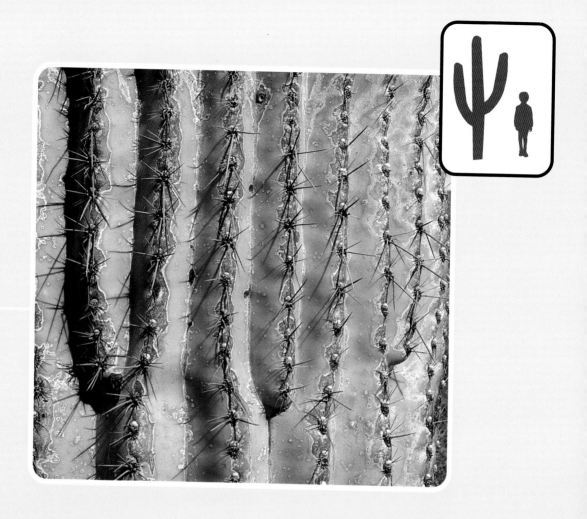

The saguaro cactus trunk and branches have **pleats** or folds. The pleats allow the saguaro to **expand** and hold a lot of rainwater. The saguaro can store enough water to last almost two years!

Barrel Cactus

The barrel cactus has some of the same
adaptations as other cactus plants. To
save water, it has spines instead of leaves.
It has **pleats** so that it can **expand** to
hold rainwater.

A barrel cactus grows faster on its northern, shadier side. This makes the whole cactus curve and point slightly to the south. People in the desert use the plant to help them find the right direction.

Joshua Tree

The Joshua tree is one of the largest **yucca** plants. Yucca plants are **evergreen** trees and shrubs **adapted** to live in the desert.

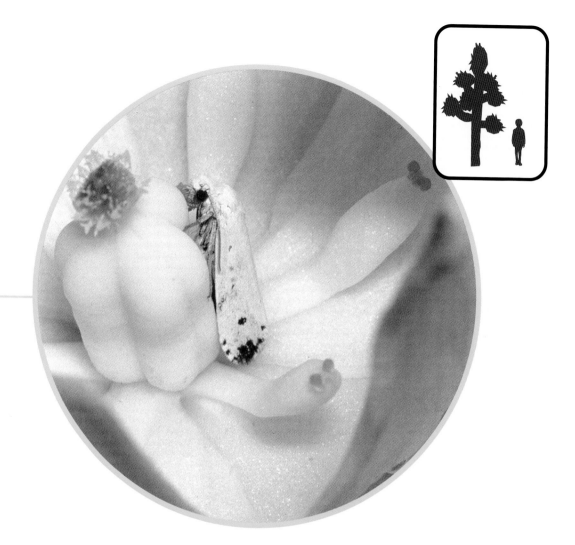

The Joshua tree and the yucca moth depend on each other for **survival.** The moth uses the **pollen** of the tree to feed its young. The moth spreads the pollen from one flower to another. This helps the Joshua tree produce seeds.

17

Sagebrush

In many desert areas, the soil is salty. The sagebrush is one of the few shrubs that can grow in salty **soil**. Sagebrush has gray-green leaves and yellow flowers that help brighten desert areas.

Sagebrush is a favorite food of many
animals. People in the desert have found
that sagebrush wood burns very quickly
and makes a hot fire.

Creosote Bush

The leaves of the creosote bush have a waxy coating that helps save water. During dry times, the large leaves fall off the plant. New, smaller leaves take their place giving the plant a better chance at **survival**.

The large creosote root system takes in
every drop of water from the ground
around the plant. This means there is
usually not enough water for other plants
to grow near the creosote bush.

21

Mexican Gold Poppy

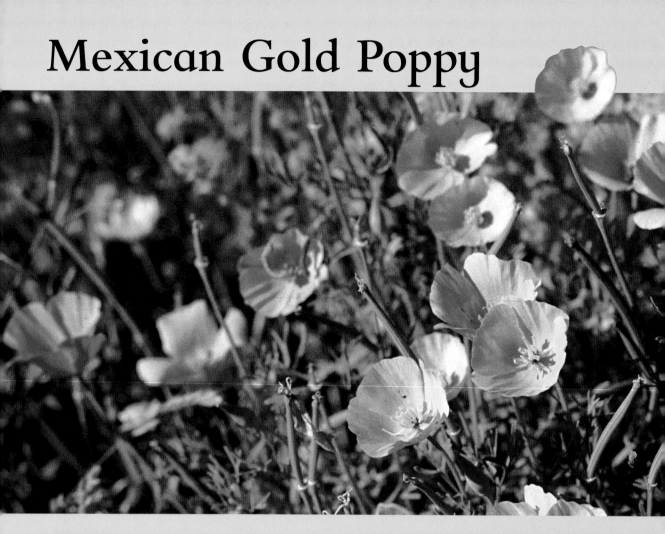

The Mexican gold poppy is one of the many **annuals** that live in the desert. An annual plant produces new plants from seeds each year.

Like other desert annuals, the Mexican gold poppy's seeds are scattered by the wind at the end of the short growing season. The seeds will **sprout** during the next rainy season.

Brittlebush

Brittlebush has bright yellow flowers.
The seeds of the brittlebush are scattered
by the wind at the end of the short
growing season.

If conditions are unusually dry or **harsh** the seeds can be **dormant** for years.

Indian Blanket

The Indian blanket plant often grows next to roads in the Southwest. The bright flower stands at the top of a thin stem.

Like many other **annuals,** the Indian blanket survives the dry season as a seed. Once the rains come, the seeds **sprout** and push through the **soil's surface.**

The Desert's Future

People used to think that nothing lived in the desert. They mined the desert for minerals. Sometimes they used the desert land to build cities. These activities have taken away some desert lands.

Some people who come to visit the desert drive off the roads. They damage fragile plants. Remember that the desert is a home to many living things—plants and animals. Treat it like you would your own home.

Glossary

adaptations changes made to meet new conditions

adapted changed to meet new conditions

annual plant that lives its entire life in one year

dormant inactive, asleep

evergreen having leaves that stay green all year long

expand make wider

fleshy thick and soft

harsh difficult or rough

pleats folds

pollen dust-size grains from flowers that help make seeds

reflect shine light back

soil ground plants grow in

sprout begin to grow

succulent having fleshy leaves

surface top part of something

survival continuing life

yucca evergreen trees and shrubs suited to live in the desert

Parts of a Plant

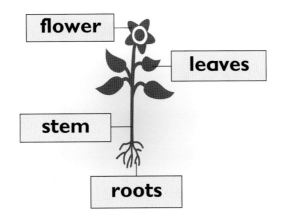

More Books to Read

Kerrod, Robin. *Plant Life*. Tarrytown, NY: Marshall Cavendish Corp. 1994.

Llamas, Andreu. *Plants of the Desert*. Broomall, PA: Chelsea House Publishers. 1996. An older reader can help you with this book.

Murray, Peter. *Deserts*. Chanhassen, MN: Child's World, Inc. 1997. An older reader can help you with this book.

O'Mara, Anna. *Deserts*. Danbury, CT: Children's Press. 1996.

Parker, Jane, & Steve Parker. *Deserts*. Danbury, CT: Franklin Watts. 1998. An older reader can help you with this book.

Index